PIONEERING COMMERCIAL CELESTIAL MINING

CHAD MANN[*]

"[W]e and other nations have a great responsibility to promote the peaceful use of space and to utilize the new knowledge obtainable from space science and technology for the benefit of all mankind."[1]

---

[*]. Juris Doctor Candidate, University of Arkansas at Little Rock, William H. Bowen School of Law ("William H. Bowen School of Law"), Class of 2017; B.A., College of the Ozarks, Point Lookout, MO. The Author is also the Chair of the William H. Bowen School of Law Moot Court Board, and a recently accepted Staff Judge Advocate with the United States Air Force. The Author thanks Professor of Law Kenneth Gallant, of the William H. Bowen School of Law. For without Professor Gallant's guidance and mentorship, this paper would not have been possible. Finally, the Author takes full responsibility for any and all errors in this work.

1. Dwight D. Eisenhower, Former President of the United States of America, Introduction to Outer Space, [iii] Statement by the President (March 26, 1958), *available at* http://history.nasa.gov/sputnik/16.html.

INTRODUCTION 3

  I.   THE PROBLEM AND SOLUTION 6

  II. THE HOW-TO AND ASSOCIATED LEGAL
       CONCERNS 8

  III. THE PRESENT LEGAL NEEDS TO
       ADDRESS FUTURE CONCENRS 20

       A. Government Incentives 20

       *B. The Need For a Worldwide Space Regulation
       and Enforcement Agency* 24

CONCLUSION 30

INTRODUCTION

Minerals are essential to humanity's modern lifestyle and have countless applications.[2] For example, the average automobile contains more than two-thousand pounds of iron and steel, two-hundred-forty pounds of aluminum, fifty pounds of carbon, forty-two pounds of copper, forty-one pounds of silicon, twenty-two pounds of zinc, and more than thirty other minerals including titanium, platinum, and gold.[3] Further, Earth's energy grid is powered by minerals, like coal-fueled power stations which produce forty-one percent of the Earth's total electricity.[4] Presently, our minerals are extracted from Earth's crust using a variety of mining techniques.[5] While Earth's crust is presently abundant in minerals, all around the world standards of living are rising which increases the demand for Earth's increased mineral extraction.[6] Also, not only is the standard of living rising around the world, but the world's human population is growing at an exponential rate.[7] For example, between 1900 and 2000 the world's human population was three times greater than humanity's entire previous history, increasing from 1.5 billion people to 6.1 billion in just one-hundred years.[8]

---

2 . Australian Government, MINERALS BASICS, History and Use, http://www.ga.gov.au/scientific-topics/minerals/basics (last visited Nov. 15, 2016).

3. United States Government Department of Geological Survey, MINERAL RESOURCE PROGRAM, Do We take Minerals for Granted?, http://minerals.usgs.gov/granted.html (last visited Nov. 15, 2016).

4. World Coal Association, COAL AND ELECTRICITY, Coal's Role in Electricity Generation Worldwide, http://www.worldcoal.org/coal/uses-coal/coal-electricity (last visited Nov. 15,2016).

5 . University of Kentucky, METHODS OF MINING, https://www.uky.edu/KGS/coal/coal_mining.htm (last visited Nov. 15, 2016).

6. United States Government Department of U.S. Geological Survey, MINERAL RESOURCE PROGRAM, Future Mineral Supplies, http://minerals.usgs.gov/granted.html#future (last visited Nov. 15, 2016).

7. Esteban Ortiz-Ospina and Max Rouser, WORLD POPULATION GROWTH (2016), https://ourworldindata .org /world- population-growth/.

8. *Id.*

According to the United Nations, Department of Economic and Social Affairs, by the year 2100 the world's total population could reach as high as 16.6 billion.[9] Coupling the exponential growth of the human population with the rising standards of living, it is clear we will need to extract increased amounts of minerals from Earth to satisfy our mineral use.[10] While one may think that due to the size of our planet such increased mineral extraction should not be an issue, one must also acknowledge that oceans cover approximately 71% of Earth's surface.[11] Further, every year each person in the United States requires more than twenty-five thousand pounds of new nonfuel minerals to make items we use every day [12] and three-hundred thirteen-million British thermal units of energy per year which amount to approximately 32,300 pounds of coal.[13] By comparing the increased demands for Earth's minerals against the inverse rate by which Earth's minerals are exhausted, some reports conclude "we will require the resources of two planets to meet

---

9. *Id.* at Uncertainty of Future Projections; *See also* United Nations Department of Economic and Social Affairs, *World Population Prospects*, https://esa.un.org/unpd/wpp/Graphs/Probabilistic/POP/TOT/ (last visited Nov. 15, 2016).
10. United States Government Department of U.S. Geological Survey, MINERAL RESOURCE PROGRAM, Future Mineral Supplies, http://minerals.usgs.gov/granted.html#future (last visited Nov. 15, 2016).
11. Michael Pidwinry, FUNDAMENTALS OF PHYSICAL GEOGRAPHY, Introduction to the Oceans (2006), http://www.physicalgeography.net/fundamentals/8o.html.
12. United States Government Department of U.S. Geological Survey, MINERAL RESOURCE PROGRAM, Future Mineral Supplies, http://minerals.usgs.gov/granted.html#future (last visited Nov. 15, 2016).
13 . United States Government Department of U.S. Energy Information Administration, FREQUENTLY ASKED QUESTIONS, How Much Energy Does a person Use in a Year? https://www.eia.gov/tools/faqs/ faq.cfm?id=85&t=1 (last visited Nov. 15, 2016).; See also United States Government Department of U.S. Energy Information Administration, FREQUENTLY ASKED QUESTIONS, HOW MUCH COAL, NATURAL GAS, OR PETROLEUM IS USED TO GENERATE A KILOWATT-HOUR OF ENERGY?, https://www.eia.gov/tools/faqs /faq.cfm?id=667&t=8 (Last visited Nov. 15, 2016).

our demands by early 2030s."[14] While the study was simply using "two planets" as a consumption guide, many scholars believe the exploitation of mineral resources from celestial bodies will soon become a necessity.[15]

While to some, the extraction of minerals from celestial bodies may sound like fiction, modern human advancements show that we are no stranger to the realm of space or its future potential. Since the former Soviet Union's successful October 1957 space launch of Sputnik I, humanity has pondered the infinite applications of space from the military, scientific, and technological developments.[16] While Sputnik I was no larger than a beach ball, its launch lead to the creation of our National Aeronautics and Space Administration ("NASA") [17] that successfully landed astronaut Neal Armstrong on the surface of the Moon in 1969.[18] Further, space is home to the International Space Station that is credited as "the most complex international scientific and engineering project in history."[19] Space is also home to other scientific and engineering feats such as the over 1,400 satellites operating in space as of July 2016.[20] On April 15, 2010, President Obama ushered in a new era of goals and challenges NASA will face in the upcoming

---

14. Psy.org, MANKIND USING EARTH'S RESOURCES AT ALARMING RATE (November 24, 2009), http://phys.org/news/2009-11-mankind-earth-resources-alarming.html.

15. 7 RICKY J. LEE, LAW AND REGULATION OF COMMERCIAL MINING OF MINERALS IN OUTER SPACE at 1 (Prof. Ram S. Jakhu ed., 2012).

16. Steve Garber, SPUTNIK AND THE DAWN OF THE SPACE AGE (Oct. 10, 2007), http://history.nasa.gov/ sputnik/.

17. *Id.*

18. United States Government Department of National Aeronautics and Space Administration, *July 20, 1969:* ONE GIANT LEAP FOR MANKIND (July 14, 2014), http://www.nasa.gov/mission_pages/apollo/ apollo11.html.

19. Tim Sharp, INTERNATIONAL SPACE STATION: FACTS, HISTORY & TRACKING (April 5, 2016), http://www.space.com/16748-international-space-station.html.

20. Union of Concerned Scientists: Science for a Healthy Planet and Safer World, UCS SATELLITE DATABASE: IN-DEPTH DETAILS ON THE 1,419 SATELLITES CURRENTLY ORBITING EARTH, http://www.ucsusa.org/nuclear-weapons/space-weapons/satellite-database#.WCZIX7IRKPO (last visited Nov. 15, 2016).

future which included answering how we are to harness minerals from distant worlds.[21] President Obama even stated that by 2025 we will send astronauts to an asteroid for the first time in history.[22]

I. THE PROBLEM AND SOLUTION

As Earth's increased mineral demands meet Earth's dwindling resources, it is no wonder our nation is looking to outer space for the solution. It is well known that various planets, moons, asteroids and other celestial bodies contain the same minerals we utilize here on Earth, and in astounding quantities.[23] For example, asteroids contain high concentrations of rare metals like gold, silver, and platinum as well as more common elements like iron and nickel.[24] Not only are asteroids potential sources of the necessary minerals we use on Earth, but they are also a richer source of the minerals as compared to Earth-based mining.[25] For example, two-thousand pounds of a mined platinum-rich asteroid may contain ten to twenty times more platinum than two-thousand pounds of mined crust from a platinum-rich location on Earth.[26] Space is home to other resources that can be invaluable in the quest to solve Earth's problems, and one of the most prominent resources is the 2009 discovery of Moon surface water.[27] Not only is

---

21. Barack Obama, President of the United States of America, Space Exploration in the 21st Century (April 15, 2010) *available at* http://www.nasa.gov/news/media/trans/obama_ksc_trans.html.
22. *Id.*
23. Massachusetts Institute of Technology, THE FUTURE OF STRATEGIC NATURAL RESOURCES, Asteroid Mining, Overview, http://web.mit.edu/12.000/www/m2016/finalwebsite/solutions/asteroids.html (last visited Nov. 15, 2016).
24. *Id.*
25. *Id.*
26. *Id.*
27. Solar System Exploration Research, NASA LOOKING TO MINE WATER ON THE MOON AND MARS, https://sservi.nasa.gov/articles/nasa-looking-to-mine-water-on-the-Moon-and-mars/ (last visited Nov. 15, 2016).

water the essence of life, but we can process it into oxygen used for breathing or use it to propel rockets further into space.[28] Also, the Moon possesses helium-3, which is nearly non-existent on Earth, that may usher in a new era of future power generation by nuclear fusion because the reaction would not produce any fast neutrons, is clean, and non-polluting.[29] Because of the vast amount of space resources, organizations like Planetary Resources and the Keck Institute for Space Studies studied the economic feasibility of extraterrestrial resource mining.[30] According to one study, the cost of returning a five-hundred-ton asteroid to low Earth orbit would cost around 2.6 billion dollars, not including the infrastructure costs to process extracted resources.[31] Further, the 2012 study posited that a single thirty-meter long platinum-rich asteroid could contain anywhere between twenty-five to fifty billion dollars' worth of platinum.[32] The study concluded that such space mining operations have the "potential for significant profit," and it is no surprise that government organizations and private companies are continually conducting feasibility studies.[33]

---

28. *Id.*
29. Paul Spudis, MINING THE MOON, http://www.americanscientist.org/bookshelf/pub/mining-the-moon (last visited Nov. 15, 2016).
30. Massachusetts Institute of Technology, *The Future of Strategic Natural Resources: Asteroid Mining*, Precedent, http://web.mit.edu/12.000/www/m2016/finalwebsite/solutions/asteroids.html (last visited Nov. 15, 2016).
31. *Id.* at Cost.
32. *Id.*
33. *Id.*

II.   THE HOW-TO AND ASSOCIATED LEGAL CONCERNS

Due to the escalating commercial interest in the field of extraterrestrial mining operations by companies like Planetary Resources,[34] Inc.; Moon Express, Inc.;[35] and Shackleton,[36] one must understand our current legal regime guiding these companies' ventures. A series of treaties negotiated before the United Nations primarily govern space law. These treaties were created after the world's leaders began negotiating outer space rules around the time the former Soviet Union launched Sputnik I into space around 1957.[37] In December 1958, the United Nations created the Office for Outer Space Affairs, which was initially created as a small unit of experts to service the ad hoc Committee on the Peaceful Uses of Outer Space.[38] The General Assembly designed the Committee on the Peaceful Uses of Outer Space to govern the exploration and use of space for humanity's benefit.[39] The Committee was instrumental in the creation of the five treaties and five

---

34. Planetary Resources, *ASTEROIDS WILL UNLOCK THE SOLAR SYSTEM'S ECONOMY*, http://www.planetaryresources.com/asteroids/#asteroids-intro (last visited Nov. 15, 2016).

35. Mike Wall, *MOON EXPRESS APPROVED FOR PRIVATE LUNAR LANDING IN 2017, A SPACE FIRST* (Aug. 03, 2016), http://www.space.com/33632-moon-express-private-lunar-landing-approval.html.

36 . Shackleton Energy, *FUELING THE SPACE FRONTIER*, http://www.shackletonenergy.com/ (last visited Nov. 15, 2016).

37. Thomas J. Herron, Note, *Deep Space Thinking: What Elon Musk's idea to Nuke Mars Teaches Us About Regulating the "Visionaries and Daredevils" of Outer Space*, 41 COLUM. J. ENVTL. L. 553, 558-585 (2016).

38 . United Nations, *OFFICE FOR OUTER SPACE AFFAIRS*, History, http://www.unoosa.org/oosa/en/aboutus/history/index.html (last visited Nov. 15, 2016).

39. United Nations, *OFFICE FOR OUTER SPACE AFFAIRS*, Committee on the Peaceful Uses of Outer Space, http://www.unoosa.org/oosa/en/ourwork/copuos/index.html (last visited Nov. 15, 2016).

principles of outer space by providing a unique platform at the global level to discuss and develop space law.[40]

Of the treaties in force, the most influential, for commercial resource extraction purposes, include the Outer Space Treaty, the Partial Test Ban Treaty, the Registration Convention, the Convention on the Prohibition of Military and Any Other Hostile Use of Environmental Modification Techniques, and the Moon Agreement. While the treaties above are exhaustive in size, their application to the commercial extraterrestrial mining operations is straightforward and simple. Article II of the Outer Space Treaty prevents states from laying territorial claims to celestial bodies so that all states may peacefully explore and use celestial bodies, including the Moon.[41] Also, Article II mandates that all activities on the Moon and other celestial bodies be conducted exclusively for peaceful purposes.[42] As applied here, commercial entities benefit from Article II because they need not appropriate budgetary provisions for space asset defense, and may focus exclusively on their mission of extracting space resources.[43]

The Test Ban Treaty forbids nuclear weapons tests or "any other nuclear explosion" in any environment, which includes outer space.[44] While one may wonder how such a ban applies to commercial space mining operations, it could significantly affect anywhere from an entity's spacecraft propulsion systems to its mining techniques. For example, in 1965 a project ran by NASA, the U.S. Air Force, and the U.S. Department of Defense was decommissioned when it was discovered that the nuclear pulse rocket technology they were

---

40. *Id.*
41. Leslie I. Tennen, Esq., *Towards a New Regime for Exploration of Outer Space Mineral Resources*, 88 NEB. L. REV. 794, 801 (2010).
42. *Id.*
43. *Id.*
44. Treaty Banning Nuclear Weapons Tests in the Atmosphere, in Outer Space and Under Water Article I, Aug. 5, 1963, 14 U.S.T. 1313, 1963 U.S.T. LEXIS 257, 14 U.S.T. 1313 [hereinafter Test Ban Treaty].

producing ran afoul the Test Ban Treaty.[45] Further, as countless domestic mining operations partake in strip mining as an efficient way to reach Earth's near-surface minerals, the practice of strip mining by explosive means may also be a viable option in space.[46]

The Registration Convention requires each launching state, sending spacecraft and other objects into space, to maintain a registry for objects launched into space to assist with identification.[47] Here, entities planning to engage in celestial mining will need to register with their state each time they send objects into space and describe what those objects are that they are sending.[48] Also, the Convention on the Prohibition of Military and Any Other Hostile Use of Environmental Modification Techniques prohibits states from "engag[ing] in military or any other hostile use of environmental modification techniques having widespread, long-lasting or severe effects as a means of destruction, damage or injury to any other State Party."[49] Article II of the treaty states the term "'environmental modification technique' refers to any technique that changes the dynamics, composition, or structure of the Earth, including its biota, lithosphere, hydrosphere and atmosphere, or outer space."[50] While it seems that the convention's prohibition superficially relates to militaristic or hostile operations meant to damage another state party, there is undoubtedly an underlying policy aimed at preserving the environments of celestial bodies. As

---

45. G.R. SCHMIDT, J.A. BONOMETTI & P.J. MORTON, *NUCLEAR PULSE PROPULSION – ORION AND BEYOND* at 7 (2000)

46. Great Mining, *Strip Mining*, http://www.greatmining.com/strip-mining.html (last visited Nov. 15, 2016).

47. The Convention on Registration of Objects Launched Into outer Space Article II, Jan. 14, 1975, 28 U.S.T. 695, 1975 U.S.T. LEXIS 552, 28 U.S.T. 695 [hereinafter Registration Treaty].

48. *Id.*

49. The Convention on the Prohibition of Military or Any Other Hostile Use of Environmental Modification Techniques Article I, May 18, 1977, 31 U.S.T. 333, 1977 U.S.T. LEXIS 427, 31 U.S.T. 333 [hereinafter Modification Convention].

50. *Id.*

applied here, commercial entities need to be cognizant as to how their mining operation affects the celestial bodies' respective environments, the pollutants of those mining operations on the celestial environments, as well as how the entity disposes of its waste.

Finally, while only non-spacefaring states accepted the Moon Agreement, it still may be a consideration to entities interested in celestial mining on the Moon.[51] One reason for the Moon Agreement being considered the least successful of the space treaties is because of the treaties prohibition on Moon mining.[52] Article 11 provides "the [M]oon and its natural resources are the common heritage of mankind.... Neither the surface nor the subsurface of the Moon, nor any part thereof or natural resources in place, shall become the property of any State, international intergovernmental or non-governmental organization, national organization or non-government entity...."[53] While the Moon Agreement expressly prohibits mining operations on the Moon, it has no binding effect on the present spacefaring states. Therefore, the Moon Agreement's only true effect is to preclude its present non-spacefaring signatories from utilizing the Moon's resources when the signatory states become spacefaring. While the treaties above do provide commercial entities some guidance as to how to conduct operations, the provisions fail to provide such specific guidance that would warrant most entities to risk time, energy, and capital exploring and developing a space mining venture. Because the present body of international space law fails to provide adequate guidance to most interested commercial entities, certain states, such as

---

51. Kyle A. Jacobsen, Comment, *From Interstate To Interstellar Commerce: Incorporating The Private Sector Into International Aerospace Law*, 87 TEMP. L. REV. 159, 169 (2014).
52. *Id.*
53. Agreement Governing the Activities of States on the Moon and Other Celestial Bodies, Article 11, Jan. 18, 1982, 1363 U.N.T.S. 21 [hereinafter Moon Agreement].

the United States, have recently taken significant strides to provide a guiding framework for its entities to operate under.

In 2015, President Obama signed the U.S. Commercial Space Launch Competitiveness Act into law.[54] The law permits United States Citizens to own any asteroid resources they extract from celestial bodies, and further encourages the commercial exploration and utilization of celestial resources.[55] Specifically, it declares that "[t]he President, acting through appropriate Federal agencies, shall...facilitate commercial exploration for and commercial recovery of space resources by United States Citizens," discourage government barriers, and "promote the right of United States Citizens to engage in commercial exploration for and commercial recovery of space resources free from harmful interference...."[56] The law promotes the commercial interest by stating:

> A United States Citizen engaged in commercial recovery of an asteroid resource or a space resource under this chapter shall be entitled to any asteroid resource or space resource obtained, including to possess, own, transport, use, and sell the asteroid resource or space resource obtained in accordance with applicable law, including the international obligations of the United States.[57]

Finally, at the end of the Act, Congress made clear that "the United States does not thereby assert sovereignty or sovereign or exclusive rights or jurisdiction over, or ownership of, any celestial

---

54. U.S. Commercial Space Launch Competitiveness Act, Pub. L. No. 114-90, 129 Stat. 704 (2015); *See also* 51 U.S.C.A. §51303 (2015).
55. *Id.* at 129 Stat. 721.
56. U.S. Commercial Space Launch Competitiveness Act, Pub. L. No. 114-90, 129 Stat. 704, 721 (2015); *See also* 51 U.S.C.A. § 51302 (2015).
57. U.S. Commercial Space Launch Competitiveness Act, Pub. L. No. 114-90, 129 Stat. 704, 721 (2015); *See also* 51 U.S.C.A. § 51303 (2015).

body."[58] During the passage of this law, Majority Leader Kevin McCarthy stated "America is a nation uniquely called to explore the final frontier... [as] we continue to lead the world in [the] advancement of technology and science."[59] McCarthy continued "The Space Act will help...unite law with innovation, allowing the next generation of pioneers to experiment, learn and succeed without being constrained by premature regulatory action."[60]

While the United States has taken great strides, far and above most other spacefaring nations, it is important to note that there is much progress to be had. Also, absent understanding the path our pioneer explorers will likely take in conducting their celestial mining operations we will not know what other strides we can take as a nation to help facilitate their adventures. Accordingly, based upon my research and belief, I think most commercial mining operations will involve eight separate stages which our lawmakers must consider separately to best facilitate the process. The stages that I will discuss in more detail in the proceeding paragraphs are as follows: planning, exploration, launch, transit to, extraction, return, processing, and transporting.

First, commercial entities are likely to engage in a planning stage whereby the entity determines what celestial bodies are best suited to explore for resources. During this stage, the predominant method of ferreting out what celestial bodies will be worthy prospects for further investigation is the use of spectrometers to determine what the celestial bodies are comprised of.[61] Spectrometers take the light signal reflecting

---

58. U.S. Commercial Space Launch Competitiveness Act, Pub. L. No. 114-90, 129 Stat. 704, 722 (2015).

59. United States Congress, *CONGRESSIONAL RECORD*, General leave, https://www.majorityleader.gov/ 2015/11/16/the-future-of-space-exploration-is-now/ (last visited Nov. 15, 2016).

60. *Id.* at {time} 1800.

61. Cornell University, *ASK AN ASTRONOMER: HOW DO WE KNOW WHAT OTHER PLANETS (AND STARS, GALAXIES, ETC.) ARE MADE OF? (INTERMEDIATE)*, http://curious.astro.cornell.edu/physics/56-our-solar-system/planets-and-dwarf-

off of the celestial body that it is focused on and spreads out the light into separate spectrums which allow scientists to compare the various light waves cast by the body to the known elements and the light that those elements can themselves emit.[62] Of course not all spectrometers work from light wavelengths, as many use infrared or x-rays, but the concept is the same and it is an efficient way to ferret out the more promising celestial bodies from the less promising celestial bodies.[63]

By now, the entity should have a fair understanding of what celestial bodies are prime targets for mining operations; however, due to the exceedingly high expense involved in developing a mining operation on a celestial body, it is likely the entity will engage in further exploration. While many celestial bodies are rich in minerals, the most prominent prospect for commercial entities is likely to be water which can be converted into liquid oxygen to fuel spacecraft in space.[64] Here, it is very likely the entity will first send robotic scouts to the most promising and financially feasible celestial bodies. The scout will likely extract core samples from the body, evaluate the samples, and transmit the data back to the entity to verify its contents much like NASA's Mars rover Curiosity has been doing since August 2012.[65] Much like NASA's current rovers, these commercial scout rovers are likely to

---

planets/general-questions/199-how-do-we-know-what-other-planets-and-stars-galaxies-etc-are-made-of-intermediate (last visited Nov. 16, 2016).
   62. *Id.*
   63. *Id.*
   64. Susan Thomas, *Gold rush in space? Asteroid miners prepare, but eye water first*, RUETERS (Nov. 21, 2013), http://www.reuters.com/article/us-space-mining-asteroids-idUSBRE9AK0JF20131121.
   65. United States Government Division of National Aeronautics and Space Administration, MARS SCIENCE LABORATORY CURIOSITY ROVER, NASA, http://mars.nasa.gov/msl/mission/overview/ (last visited Nov. 16, 2016).

remain on the celestial body and continually scour the celestial body for further resources until their operational life comes to an end.[66]

After receiving the scout's data, mapping the same, and determining which part of the celestial body is best suited for a mining operation to harvest resources, commercial entities will likely soon plan the launch phase. At the early stages of the celestial resource mining era, most launches are likely to take place from Earth; whereas, later in the celestial resource mining era most commercial entities are likely to have substantial complexes on the Moon due to the reduced cost of leaving the Moon's low gravity field.[67] Currently, it costs the United States approximately $225 million per launch to enter low Earth orbit, but as technology advances those costs are expected fall.[68] Presently, all launches within the United States must register with the Federal Aviation Administration ("FAA"), and abide by all FAA regulations and policies.[69]

After liftoff comes the waiting stage—transit to the celestial body. Transit to the celestial body can take a significant amount of time, as a standard trip to Mars takes approximately six to eight months,[70] but closer celestial bodies take a fraction of that time, such as a standard

---

66. United States Government Division of National Aeronautics and Space Administration, *MARS EXPLORATION*, NASA, http://mars.nasa.gov/mer10/ (last visited Nov. 16, 2016).

67. Dr. David R. Williams, *MOON FACT SHEET*, NASA (April 19, 2016) http://nssdc.gsfc.nasa.gov/ planetary/factsheet/moonfact.html; *See also* University of Illinois, *DEPARTMENT OF PHYSICS*, Illinois.edu (Oct. 22, 2007), https://van.physics.illinois.edu/qa/listing.php?id=1018.

68. United Launch Alliance, *FREQUENTLY ASKED QUESTIONS – LAUNCH COSTS*, http://www.ulalaunch. com/faqs-launch-costs.aspx (last visited Nov. 16, 2016).

69. Federal Aviation Administration, *LAUNCH OR REENTRY VEHICLES*, FAA, https://www.faa.gov/ about/office_org/headquarters_offices/ast/licenses_permits/launch_reentry/ (last visited Nov. 16, 2016).

70. United States Government Division of National Aeronautics and Space Administration, *HOW LONG WOULD A TRIP TO MARS TAKE*, NASA, http://image.gsfc.nasa.gov/poetry/venus/q2811.html (last visited Nov. 16, 2016).

trip to the Moon taking only around three days.[71] The main asteroid belt, consisting of the vast majority of asteroids in our solar system, lies between Mars and Jupiter, and recent trips to the main belt have taken anywhere from less than three months to around four and a half months.[72] The travel times to celestial bodies are confusing because the unique trips must account for the planetary position at launch, the receiving celestial body's position, and the trajectory the craft must take to account for both celestial bodies' respective orbits. While the main asteroid belt is quite far from Earth, fortunately, another significant source of minerals celestial mining pioneers can utilize are various classes of Near Earth Asteroids.[73] There are three classifications of Near Earth Asteroids, and two of the three classes cross Earth's orbit, placing them, at times, closer to Earth than any other celestial body.[74] Summarily, no matter the celestial body of choice, the wait time as the mining units arrive at the destination is time-consuming. Presently the average orbital space shuttle travels at around 17,500 miles per hour,[75] but as technological developments in space travel continue to evolve faster travel speeds will reduce travel time to celestial bodies.

---

71. Brett Smith, *WHAT IS THE QUICKEST ROUTE TO THE MOON & HOW LONG DOES IT TAKE?*, seattlepi, http://education.seattlepi.com/quickest-route-moon-long-take-6233.html (last visited Nov. 16, 2016).

72. Matt Williams, *HOW LONG DOES IT TAKE TO GET TO THE ASTEROID BELT?*, Universe Today (Aug. 10, 2016), http://www.universetoday.com/130231/long-take-get-asteroid-belt/.

73. Spaceguard Foundation, *NEAR EARTH ASTEROIDS*, Spaceguard, http://spaceguard.rm.iasf.cnr.it/ NScience/neo/neo-what/ast-neas.htm (last visited Nov. 16, 2016).

74. Vanderbilt University, *ASTEROIDS*, Vanderbilt, http://www.vanderbilt.edu/AnS/physics/astrocourses/ AST101/readings/asteroids.html (last visited Nov. 16, 2016).

75. United States Government Division of National Aeronautics and Space Administration, *SPACE SHUTTLE AND INTERNATIONAL SPACE STATION*, NASA, http://www.nasa.gov/centers/kennedy/ about/information/shuttle_faq.html#14 (last visited Nov. 16, 2016).

When the mining units arrive at the celestial body, the celestial mining operation will commence. It is highly unlikely celestial mining operations will involve human laborers; rather, the mining is expected to be carried out by robots due to the inherent risks the space environment coupled with dangers the mining process presents.[76] After all, since robotic mining is well established on Earth,[77] and some studies say 96% of those non-automated mining jobs can be automated,[78] it should be no surprise that the celestial mining pioneers will utilize the automated process in their operations afar. The celestial mining pioneers will face unique problems in mining celestial bodies such as asteroids because of the asteroids' reduced mass. It is because of this reduced mass that the structures have very limited gravity which may require mining techniques to keep the mining equipment fastened to the asteroid and unique capture techniques to keep the mined mineral from floating off the asteroid and into deep space.[79] While miners will likely use techniques similar to those utilized here on Earth, the celestial mining process is likely to be significantly slower than Earth's mining process due to the mining equipment being solar powered with limited operational time.[80] However, rather than exclusively solar power, the United Nations postulates "that for some missions in outer space nuclear power sources are particularly suited or even essential owning

---

76. United States Government Division of National Aeronautics and Space Administration, THE HUMAN BODY IN SPACE, NASA, http://www.nasa.gov/hrp/bodyinspace (last visited Nov. 16, 2016).
77. Evan Ackerman, *NASA Training 'Swarmie' Robots for Space* Mining, IEEE (Aug. 20, 2014), http://spectrum.ieee.org/automaton/robotics/military-robots/nasa-training-swarmie-robots-for-space-mining.
78. Frik Els, STUDY SHOWS 96% OF SOME MINING JOBS CAN BE AUTOMATED, MINING.com (Dec. 22, 2015) http://www.mining.com/study-shows-96-of-some-mining-jobs-can-be-automated/.
79. Kevin Bonsor, *HOW ASTEROID MINING WILL WORK*, HowStuffWorks.com (Nov. 10, 2000), http://science.howstuffworks.com/asteroid-mining2.htm.
80. *Id.*

their compactness, long life and other attributes."[81] Whatever the method of extracting the resource, after the resources are extracted they must be loaded into a transportation shuttle for their return trip to a mineral processing facility.

After the transportation shuttle is loaded with the raw mined celestial resources, the shuttle will depart the celestial body and to a processing facility where the raw materials will be broken down into the respective materials—the return phase. While we currently process all of our raw materials and resources on Earth, I propose that such processing should take place on the Moon. By processing resources on the Moon, it prevents mineral processing waste from spilling into Earth's atmosphere, and since the Moon's atmosphere is nearly nonexistent, the entry into the Moon's atmosphere will be easier on the delivering shuttles.[82] For Earth-based operations, the transit home is likely to be more challenging because Earth's dense atmosphere causes objects entering Earth to burn as they collide with the closely packed molecules held by Earth's high gravity due to extremely high level of friction.[83] Further, re-entry into Earth's atmosphere is complicated as an entering shuttle barreling toward Earth at too steep of an angle could cause increased friction causing a greater chance the entry vehicle could burn up, and a shuttle's entry being too shallow could cause the vehicle to skip across the atmosphere and bounce back into orbit.[84] As for Moon based operations, such landing considerations are moot due to the

---

81. WORLD NUCLEAR ASSOCIATION, *NUCLEAR REACTORS AND RADIOISOTOPES FOR SPACE,* world-nuclear.org (Feb. 2016), http://www.world-nuclear.org/information-library/non-power-nuclear-applications/transport/ nuclear-reactors-for-space.aspx.

82. Opik, E. J., *THE DENSITY OF THE LUNAR ATMOSPHERE,* 4(6) IRISH ASTRONOMICAL JOURNAL, 186, 189 (1959)

83. Massachusetts Institute of Technology, *ASK AN ENGINEER: WHY DON'T SPACECRAFT BURN UP OR VEER OFF COURSE DURING REENTRY FROM SPACE?*, MIT (Oct. 16, 2012), http://engineering.mit.edu/ask/why-don%E2%80%99t-spacecraft-burn-or-veer-course-during-reentry-space.

84. *Id.*

thin atmosphere being equal to that which currently surrounds the International Space Station.[85]

While the final two stages of the celestial mining operation, processing the raw resources and transporting the processed resources to Earth, are each unique and involve separate components, they are so intertwined it will suffice for this paper's purpose to discuss them simultaneously. The processing of the raw extracted celestial resources should be no stranger to modern mining, but perhaps we will see such operations take place on other celestial bodies due to the pollution and health considerations the processing operations presently pose to the Earth.[86] Further, if entities begin smelting operations on the Moon, or other celestial bodies, it will dramatically increase potential profits per trip to the Earth. For example, imagine two transportation vessels, one possessing refined materials ready to be sold at market, and the other possessing raw resources. Both vessels undergo the expense of launching, returning to Earth, and undergoing repairs due to the damage the vessels sustain upon reentry. However, the vessel with the unrefined resources will yield far less profit as it is unlikely the post processing waste resources will be sold on any market, whereas the vessel with the refined resource can sell its entire payload.

---

85. United States Government Division of National Aeronautics and Space Administration, IS THERE AN ATMOSPHERE ON THE MOON?, NASA, https://www.nasa.gov/mission_pages/LADEE/news/lunar-atmosphere.html (last visited Nov. 16, 2016).
86. BLACKSMITH INSTITUTE, METALS SMELTERS AND PROCESSING, Worstpolluted.org, http://www.worstpolluted.org/projects_reports/display/61 (last visited Nov. 16, 2016).

III. PRESENT LEGAL NEEDS TO ADDRESS FUTURE CONCERNS

A. *Government Incentives*

Government incentives are powerful driving forces that motivate and enable corporations and individuals to engage in seemingly risky endeavors. For example, The Homestead Act of 1862 provided American citizens powerful incentives to colonize the western frontier. The Homestead Act of 1862 was such a powerful incentive it is credited with over 1.6 million homestead applications being filed, and more than 270 million acres of the western frontier passed into the hands of individuals.[87] Arguably, the second most relevant successful government incentive was The Pacific Railway Act, signed into law by former President Abraham Lincoln on July 1, 1862.[88] The Pacific Railway Act of 1862 provided government support for the construction of the first transcontinental railroad.[89] The passage of The Pacific Railway Act of 1862 is hailed as "one of the greatest technological achievements of the 19th century,"[90] and it supported the settlement of

---

87. United States Government Division of National Archives, NATIONAL ARCHIVES: THE HOMESTEAD ACT OF 1862, https://www.archives.gov/education/lessons/homestead-act (last visited Nov. 16, 2016).

88. United States Government Library of Congress, WEB GUIDES BY THE LIBRARY OF CONGRESS DIGITAL REFERENCE SECTION: PRIMARY DOCUMENTS IN AMERICAN HISTORY, The Library of Congress, https://www.loc.gov/rr/program/bib/ourdocs/PacificRail.html (last visited Nov. 16, 2016).

89. *Id.*

90. United States government Senate, *United States Senate: Landmark Legislation:* THE PACIFIC RAILWAY ACT OF 1862, http://www.senate.gov/artandhistory/history/common/generic/PacificRailwayActof1862.htm (last visited Nov. 16, 2016).

the western colonies by providing an easy means to transport needed materials.[91]

Unlike the Pacific Railway Act of 1862 that ushered in the "iron arms" of rail, International law and domestic efforts to encourage space pioneers fall short of the requisite motivation level and guidance necessary to provoke most space pioneers. In 1862, rail, as a means of transportation into the western territories of the United States, was considered "like a skilled magician" that "most firmly established institutions of man" and rescued the western colonies "from the primitive wilderness."[92] While far from primitive, Space is analogous to the west in 1862 in that Space is predominantly an uninhabited region with countless variables, unknowns, and presently extremely limited access. Like how The Pacific Railway Act of 1862 helped to extend access to the west, the United States has been sending billions of dollars to Boeing and SpaceX to restore United States independence in space access, and help entities other than the government to have a routine means of accessing space.[93]

Further, while NASA had a shuttle fleet regularly used to reach the International Space Station, the shuttle program was disbanded by the Bush Administration in 2010 when former President Bush announced a new sweeping "vision for space exploration."[94] This new vision required shifting NASA's budget from the shuttle program to fund the new Constellation program without increasing NASA's

---

91. Charles A. Schwantes, TRANSCONTINENTAL RAILROAD: HOW RAILROADS TOOK THE 'WILD' OUT OF THE WEST, Historynet.com, http://www.historynet.com/transcontinental-railroad (last visited Nov. 16, 2016).
92. *Id.*
93. Greg White, SPACE.NEWS: NASA AWARDS SPACEX CONTRACT TO SEND ASTRONAUTS TO ISS AND RESTORE AMERICAN INDEPENDENCE, SPACE.news (Dec. 10, 2015), http://www.space.news/2015-11-24-nasa-awards-spacex-contract-to-send-astronauts-to-iss-and-restore-american-independence.html.
94. John Schwartz, THE NEW YORK TIMES: ONE WAY UP: U.S. SPACE PLAN RELIES ON RUSSIA, NYTimes (Oct. 5, 2008), http://www.nytimes.com/2008/10/06/science/space/06gap.html.

already seventeen billion dollars annually appropriated for its budget. While the United States is said to be dependent on Russia to reach the ISS until 2018, and possibly as late as 2019,[95] NASA is presently designing the Orion Spacecraft that is said to "provide an entirely new national capability for human exploration beyond Earth's orbit."[96] While the Orion Spacecraft sounds promising in its development, we still have yet to see the United States put forth sufficient efforts to establish a present day "iron arms" means of transportation to space to facilitate its research and development. While we see the United States incentivizing companies like Boeing and SpaceX to boost their near Earth orbit capabilities, and the United States using NASA's unmatched expertise to develop greater technologies to continue to lead at the forefront of the World's space exploration, we still fall short of the of the incentives necessary to enable entities to "firmly establish" space mining operations.[97]

Much like the Homestead Act of 1862, the passage of the U.S. Commercial Space Launch Competitiveness Act does motivate space pioneers to reach into space and lay claim to resources harvested from celestial bodies; however, the Homestead Act of 1862 provided sure title to 160 acres of western lands if the settlers improved and cultivated the lands for five years, whereas the U.S. Commercial Space Launch Competitiveness Act only provides an ownership interest in the resources extracted from the celestial body.[98] Absent the guarantee of a

---

95. Ledyard King, *USATODAY: NASA to keep paying Russia to send astronauts to space station*, USA TODAY (Aug. 5, 2015), http://www.usatoday.com/story/news/nation/2015/08/05/nasa-keep-paying-russia-send-astronauts-space-station/31178519/.
96 . Charles Bolden, *WHAT'S NEXT FOR NASA?*, NASA (May 24, 2016), http://www.nasa.gov/about/ whats_next.html.
97. *Id.*
98. United States Government Library of Congress, *WEB GUIDES BY THE LIBRARY OF CONGRESS DIGITAL REFERENCE SECTION: PRIMARY DOCUMENTS IN AMERICAN HISTORY*, The Library of Congress,

fixed area of land, the space mining pioneers cannot ensure that their expense of planning, exploring, launching, transporting, and extracting their resources will not be exploited by another entity or state when the other entity or state arrives at the same celestial body and begins extracting resources in the same vicinity. Such a disturbance in a mining pioneers operation could transform the desired peaceful space mining era into a modern day gold rush whereby we experience overcrowded mining operations potentially leading to conflicts over prime celestial mining territory.[99]

Summarily, while the United States is providing some incentives, such as the funding provided to Boeing and SpaceX to develop their low Earth orbit capabilities, its incentives are short of the incentives provided in the Pacific Railway Act of 1862, and Homestead Act of 1862. Despite the efforts, United States incentives still leave ample room for the space pioneers to debate whether or not the risky venture into space wilderness will be successful and peaceful or will amount to a gold-rush style frenzy. I advocate that while we can do more to motivate the space mining pioneers, the United States should form an agency comprised of other spacefaring nations to promulgate necessary rules and regulations and serve as the worldwide enforcement authority of those regulations.

---

https://www.loc.gov/rr/program/bib/ourdocs/Homestead.html (last visited Nov. 16, 2016).
   99. A&E Television Networks, LLC, *HISTORY: THE GOLD RUSH OF 1849*, http://www.history.com/ topics/gold-rush-of-1849 (last visited Nov. 16, 2016).

B. *The Need For a Worldwide Space Regulation and Enforcement Agency*

The World's spacefaring nations developing a worldwide space regulation and enforcement agency would best serve countless necessary roles unique to space mining industry. First, the enforcement agency must serve as a primary enforcer to the regulations it promulgates for the space mining industry. For example, suppose a company named MannPower Electric was extracting H3 from the Moon, and while its mining units left the extraction site to refuel, Intruder Industries' mining bots trespassed on MannPower's dig site, and began extracting minerals. Presently, there is no property interest MannPower could assert to lay claim to the land that is occupied by Intruder's mining bots, but it is clear that the World's regulation and enforcement agency needs to pass and enforce limited territorial claims to prevent potential conflict. Further, assuming arguendo that such a regulation did exist, and that Intruder's trespass was a violation of MannPower's property interest, the enforcement agency could take whatever steps necessary to ensure MannPower is restored possession of its dig site and compensated for any resulting damage. Absent a worldwide regulation-making body, and a branch enforcing the regulations, space mining pioneers risk loss in their mining endeavors without an enforceable worldwide remedy against wrongdoers.

International law presently lacks a worldwide agency to promulgate, oversee, and enforce space regulations. Here in the United States, Section 108 of the U.S. Commercial Space Launch Competitiveness Act calls for recommendations to regulatory approaches that would best "prioritize safety, utilize existing authorities, minimize burdens to the industry, promote the U.S. Commercial space sector, and meet the United States obligations under international treaties...."¹⁰⁰ On Section 108's face, it may indicate the United States' intent to develop a purely domestic regulatory agency. Further, the U.S. Commercial Space Launch Competitiveness Act hints at this purely domestic regulatory agency in Section 111 where it states in year 2023 "the Secretary [of Transportation] may propose regulations...[and] such regulations shall take into consideration the evolving standards of the commercial space flight industry...."¹⁰¹ While the United States regulatory agencies have undoubtedly been successful in countless fields, may claim that American industry is over-regulated.¹⁰² Further, some claim that as a result of such over-regulation, industries leave the United States and develop their companies abroad.¹⁰³

It is clear that space-related activities, like celestial mining operations, carry with them an inherent risk due to the dangers unique to the space industry. For example, on September 1, 2016, SpaceX's 604-ton Falcon 9 Rocket exploded during a test firing, and in June 2015, another SpaceX Falcon 9 rocket exploded only minutes after liftoff destroying one-hundred and ten million dollars in cargo for the International Space Station.¹⁰⁴ While no injuries were reported in either Falcon 9 explosions, the space industry has before taken lives, and most notably so on January 28, 1986, when the American space shuttle

---

100. U.S. Commercial Space Launch Competitiveness Act, Pub. L. No. 114-90, 129 Stat. 704, 707-08 (2015).

101. U.S. Commercial Space Launch Competitiveness Act, Pub. L. No. 114-90, 129 Stat. 704, 709-11 (2015); *See also* 51 U.S.C.A. § 50905 (2015).

102. The Economist Newspaper, THE ECONOMIST: OVER-REGULATED AMERICA, (Feb. 18, 2012), http://www.economist.com/node/21547789.

103. Congressman Ted Poe, HUMAN EVENTS: EPA REGULATIONS STRANGLING AMERICA, (Apr. 25, 2011), http://humanevents.com/2011/04/25/epa-regulations-strangling-america/.

104. Samantha Masunaga and Jim Puzzanghera, LOS ANGELES TIMES: SPACEX EXPLOSION FRUSTRATES BOTH ELON MUSK'S AND MARK ZUCKERBERG'S PLANS, LATimes.com (Sep. 1, 2016), http://www.latimes.com/business/la-fi-space-x-explosion-20160901-snap-story.html.

Challenger exploded only seventy-three seconds after liftoff, killing all aboard.[105] Also on February 1, 2003, the space shuttle Columbia disintegrated upon reentry into Earth's atmosphere also killing all aboard.[106] Because of the risks associated with the space industry, certain regulations must be created and enforced to ensure safe operations, but such regulations should not be so burdensome or complicated so as to impede space pioneer's efforts. Finally, absent a worldwide coalition of spacefaring nations forming a joint agency, space pioneers could move their operations to states enforcing fewer regulations to reduce cost. To best facilitate the needs for efficient safety regulations, and prevent space pioneers from simply relocating its operations to mitigate regulation compliance expense, spacefaring nations should work together to create an agency that creates space regulations, oversees the worldwide space industry, and enforces the regulations around the globe.

Further, the enforcement agency would need to track and restrict the amount of minerals imported into Earth's market to avoid crashing markets. For example, around mid-2014 a barrel of oil valued a little above $100 per barrel, but since then, domestic production of oil has nearly doubled, and due to the increase in engine efficiency of modern automobiles the oil demand has slowed.[107] Accordingly, as there is more supply of oil, and less demand, simple economics show that prices are likely to fall—as the oil prices are presently around $44 per barrel.[108] Like crude oil, any space resource introduced into the world

---

105. A&E Television Networks, LLC, *HISTORY: CHALLENGER DISASTER*, History.com, http://www.history.com/topics/challenger-disaster (last visited Sep. 22, 2016).
106. *Id.*
107. Clifford Krauss, *NEW YORK TIMES: OIL PRICES: WHAT'S BEHIND THE VOLATILITY? SIMPLE ECONOMICS*, NYTimes (Nov. 02, 2016), http://www.nytimes.com/interactive/2016/business/energy-environment/oil-prices.html?_r=0.
108. *Id.*

economy will increase the availability of the resource, and potentially lower the value of the resource accordingly. By analogy, platinum is the most expensive metal on Earth and the world harvested around 178 metric tons of platinum in 2015.[109] The mere 178 metric tons of platinum pales in comparison to an asteroid seen passing Earth around July of 2015 that is said to contain "90 million metric tons of platinum and other precious metals."[110] A spontaneous introduction of such a vast amount of resources into the market is likely to have a catastrophic effect on the markets, but if a regulation agency slowly introduced the harvested minerals into the market, it could prevent the markets from drastically crashing, and would also lower the price of the metals which would benefit countless industries utilizing the resources. Finally, as the regulation agency would need to serve as the venue by which space mining entities funnel resources into the market, the entity importing the resources could also be charged a tariff should the agency choose to do so.

With the agency serving as the central hub whereby space resources are introduced into the world markets, it can also hear and decide issues on conflicts between entities as it relates to issues of space law. Undoubtedly, multiple space pioneers from different states will need to work together as they enter into new worlds and develop the galactic mining era. Accordingly, there is no better forum to serve as an arbitrator for space issues than the agency responsible for space enforcement. Presently, Section 106 of the U.S. Space Launch Competitiveness Act declares that "[a]ny claim by a third party or space flight participant for death, bodily injury, or property damage or loss

---

109. Patricia J. Loferski, MINERAL RESOURCE PROGRAM: PLATINUM-GROUP METALS, U.S. Geological Survey, http://minerals.usgs.gov/minerals/pubs/commodity/platinum/mcs-2016-plati.pdf (last visited Nov. 16, 2016).

110. Robert Hacket, FORTUNE: ASTEROID PASSING CLOSE TO EARTH COULD CONTAIN $5.4 TRILLION OF PRECIOUS METALS, FORTUNE (July 20, 2015), http://fortune.com/2015/07/20/asteroid-precious-metals/.

resulting from an activity carried out under the license shall be the exclusive jurisdiction of the Federal Courts."[111] With all due respect to our honorable federal courts, the primary issue with space law matters litigating before the federal courts arises when a party to the matter is beyond the reach of our federal court system. Even with a declaratory judgment, absent the ability to reach the wrongdoer or the wrongdoer's assets, the claimant may not receive the remedy sought. Finally, by the agency consisting of all spacefaring nations the agency will not only be able to serve as a worldwide forum for litigating space issues, but it will also likely increase the chance that the agency will be able to reach wrongdoers and hale them into court.

The regulatory agency also needs to oversee the space mining pioneers' operations to ensure they are not running afoul The Registration Convention's mandates requiring any space mining operation not to alter the dynamics of any celestial body. As mining is known to impact the Earth's environment, we should expect similar environmental impacts abroad.[112] As mining is likely to affect celestial bodies' environments, I propose that the enforcement agency retains the power to place progressive tariffs on non-complying celestial mining entities that increase at regular intervals until the entity comes within compliance of the violated regulation. Otherwise, I advocate we dissolve the registration convention to the extent it applies to asteroids and the Moon, as the effective production of celestial minerals will be a giant challenge absent celestial environment concerns that are unlikely to affect Earth and its atmosphere.

Finally, the regulation agency needs to be the central location whereby all space operations are monitored, much like the airspace and air traffic management that the Federal Aviation Administration

---

111. U.S. Commercial Space Launch Competitiveness Act, Pub. L. No. 114-90, 129 Stat. 704, 707 (2015); *See also* 51 U.S.C.A. § 50914 (2015).

112 . Michael J. McKinley, *POLLUTION ISSUES: MINING*, Pollution Issues, http://www.pollutionissues.com/Li-Na/Mining.html (last visited Nov. 16, 2016).

administers.[113] Space traffic management may seem like an unmanageable task, but it is a task that must be had due to the exceedingly expensive and sensitive instruments presently, and to be, in space. For example, consider the International Space Station; the most expensive human-made object ever built—having cost approximately $160 billion.[114] This exceedingly expensive creation orbits Earth at five miles per second (17,150 miles per hour).[115] Now imagine how catastrophic it would be if space traffic went unregulated and one lone mining drone crashed into the International Space Station on its voyage to investigate a potentially promising asteroid. The damage would be catastrophic and could cost lives considering the International Space Station presently hosts five astronauts.[116] Section 109 of the U.S. Commercial Space Launch Competitiveness Act orders a study of space traffic and orbital actives and calls for a recommendation as to the most "appropriate framework for the protection of the health, safety, and welfare of the public and economic vitality of the space industry."[117] While the study is a great first step into what framework will be most appropriate, the section focuses primarily on United States government assets and United States private sector assets and fails to acknowledge the need for a worldwide agency.

---

113 . United States Government Federal Aviation Administration, FEDERAL AVIATION ADMINISTRATION: WHAT WE DO, FAA, https://www.faa.gov/about/mission/activities/ (last visited Nov. 16, 2016).

114. Investopedia LLC, INVESTOPEDIA: WHAT'S THE MOST EXPENSIVE MAN-MADE OBJECT EVER BUILT?, INVESTOPEDIA (Apr. 29, 2015), http://www.investopedia.com/ask/answers/042915/whats-most-expensive-manmade-object-ever-built.asp.

115. IPAC, COOL COSMOS: HOW FAST DOES THE SPACE STATION TRAVEL?, Cool Cosmos, http://coolcosmos.ipac.caltech.edu/ask/282-How-fast-does-the-Space-Station-travel- (last visited Nov. 16, 2016).

116 . Brad Eshbach, HOW MANY PEOPLE ARE IN SPACE RIGHT NOW?, http://www.howmanypeopleareinspacerightnow.com/ (last visited Nov. 16, 2016).

117. U.S. Commercial Space Launch Competitiveness Act, Pub. L. No. 114-90, 129 Stat. 704, 708-09 (2015).

Conclusion

Space mining may seem like an unreachable fiction, but it may be our only way to maintain our rising standards of living with the exponential growth of our human population. Modern advancements in space technology prove our society is no longer stranger to space; rather, space is home to many carrying out missions at the International Space Station, home to over 1,400 satellites, and home to numerous rovers exploring lands afar. While international law provides some guidance for our space mining pioneers, to best facilitate the space mining pioneers, the spacefaring nations of the world must work together to promulgate, oversee, and enforce a new efficient legal framework that mitigates space industry dangers, and takes the uncertainty out of the space mining venture. Finally, the United States must further facilitate commercial entities' space mining ventures through various government incentives because—as Earth's leading space authority—we have a duty to use our expertise for the better of all humanity. As former President John Kennedy stated in 1961, "[n]ow it is time to take longer strides—time for a great new American enterprise—time for this nation to take a clearly leading role in space achievement, which in many ways may hold the key to our future on [E]arth."[118]

---

118. John F. Kennedy, former President of the United States of America, The Goal of Sending a Man to the Moon IX. Space (May 25, 1961), *available at* http://millercenter.org/president/speeches/speech-3368.